CAMBRIDGE LEARNING HOUSE

Cambridge Learning House
71-75 Shelton Street,
Covent Garden,
London,
England, WC2H 9JQ

Find us on Social Media @CambridgeLearningHouse

For all those of us who suffered during 2020.
May it make us stronger.

Winter 2020:
Rain and Fire

New Year's Eve celebrations around the world opened the door to what many would hope to be a prosperous, fulfilling, and enlightening new year. Whilst the beginning of the new decade, the 20's, began with optimism for many it also opened with military assassinations, a plethora of fatal natural disasters and the emerging awareness of a potential coronavirus crises on the horizon.

As the 1st January dawned and Scots were celebrating the victory of Peter Wright winning the **Worlds Darts Championship** the United States sent military troops to the Middle East to deter pro-Iranian protesters who had sieged the US Embassy in Baghdad. The fire-lighting activists were responding in retaliation to a series of airstrikes by the U.S embassy which had killed 24 members of an Iranian-backed Militia over the weekend. In turn, the US air strikes had been launched in order to respond to the killing of an American contractor who was killed in an Iranian launched attack on an Iraqi military base only days before. This ping-ponging of revenge attacks was followed only two days later a US led drone strike which killed the top Iranian security commander

General Qasem Solemani outside of Baghdad airport. A death widely reported as an US military **assassination** of the Iranian commander who had been accused of planning attacks on American diplomats. 2020, had begun with the vain of deadly destruction it would set out to continue by both man and the earth, fire, wind, and sea of natural forces. As such politically charged assassinations continued to rile up the relationship between the US and certain Middle Eastern states, Australia began the year continuing to battle the **unruly bushfires** that had been devastating the nation for weeks in the run up to the new year. Known as the 'Black Summer', these wildfires were decimating over 165,000 square miles of the country whilst simultaneously, pint-sized Australian pop princess, Kylie Minogue starred in an international television campaign by Tourism Australia to encourage the world to visit these very areas. The fires which lasted until March 2020 were likely caused by drought and Climate Change and cost the Australian government more than $100 billion according to some estimates. On the 4th January 2020, Australian Prime Minister, Scott Morrison was one of the first world leaders of the year to be heavily criticised, for one reason or another, as the Australian population blamed his poor leadership for the failure of the emergency services to have eliminated over 200 fires across the country before the year had begun.

It wasn't only Australia who began the year battling nature, as mother earth brought its devastation to one side of the planet, over on the South American continent, Puerto Rico greeted 2020 with significant damage as a **magnitude 6.4 earthquake** rocked the nation on January 7th, displacing 8000 from their damaged homes, killing one person and injuring many others. The earthquake was the latest in a series of previously minor earthquakes which had shook the country since the year began. The US were amongst the first to support offering $5million of emergency aid, with the cost to Puerto Rico themselves in excess of $2 million, a burden which would soon only minor with the events which 2020 would later bring to the nation.

Suggesting political assassinations, rebellious wildfires and unceasing earthquakes were not enough to settle 2020s thirst for mortality in the first weeks of January, the world was awoken on the 8th to discover that **Ukrainian Airlines, Flight 752 had plummeted to the ground in flames**. An event bringing short the life of 176 individuals from a variety of nations. The needless waste of such human life became apparent as Iranian officials confirmed they had unintentionally shot down the passenger jet with one of their own missiles in response to a 'human error', which Iranian President Hassan Rouhani later described as a 'disastrous mistake'. Flight 752 had taken off from Imam Khomeini International airport in Tehran, during the early hours of the morning, only to be engulfed in flames, crashing minutes after take-off from a height of approximately, 8000 feet. Coming at a time when tensions between Iran and neighbours was high, Iranian state media initially denied any Iranian involvement in the crash before officials eventually took ownership of the fatal tragedy and confessed their nations unfortunate error, citing the plane as having been mistaken for a 'hostile' craft near their airspace. Unsurprisingly, the Ukrainian Airlines crash coupled with its connections to Iranian tensions dominated much of the world's media for the second week of January, yet there was news emerging in China at the time receiving much less attention; the discovery of a new form of Coronavirus which had linked to cases of a rapidly spreading form of **'viral pneumonia' in Wuhan**. This was news which would have much more significance than the world's population were ready to appreciate at the time.

As January progressed, suspected cases of a new form of coronavirus appeared in Thailand, Korea and Japan in individuals who had recently travelled to the Wuhan province of China. By the 20th, the Chinese National Health Commission had confirmed that the virus was indeed transferable from human to human leading to Wuhan's eventual suspension of any public transport which took people out of the region where cases of the virus were escalating. The city of Wuhan in Hubei province China would soon proceed from a little known Chinese urban populous to a city known by nations of people all over the world.

As January drew to an end, the world's sporting

enthusiasts grieved one of the world's greatest basketball players, Kobe Bryant, reaching a tragically early conclusion to his life as his **helicopter crashed** in foggy conditions in the hills of California. Along with other victims on board, was his 13-year-old daughter. This death of a celebrity was followed by the deaths of a further 70 unknowns in Southeast Brazil as January's murderous death toll soured as **tragic landslides and floods** swept engulfed the country, resulting in the displacement of over 45,000 people from their homes in the states around Rio de Janeiro.

After a grim month of nature and human induced unnecessarily fatality, January drew to an end on the 31st. The day the United Kingdom's formally **withdrew from the European Union**, signalling the beginning of the end of a process which had socially and politically divided the UK population for the past four years.

The Spread of Terror

Arguably one of the most depressing years ever noted in recent human history, 2020 ensured it would do its best to offer maximum scope for tragedy by shoehorning in one extra day at the end of February as a leap year day. This bonus extension of 2020 came at the end of a month which began with another rare date, Palindrome day. 02/02/2020 was the first date which read the same forwards as it did backwards for 909 years since 11th November 1111. This unique day also landed on another palindrome, the 33rd day of the year. Spookily enough, due to the additional date of February 29th being added to 2020 Palindrome Day left a remaining 333 days, another palindrome, for 2020 to unleash more terror ahead. Characterised by a global spread of both shootings, Coronavirus and a plethora of climate related phenomena, February 2020 began with a **plague of millions of locusts** spreading across Eastern Africa, decimating arable crops and threatening the food supplies of millions of people across Somalia. The infestation eventually spread south into Kenya and further westwards into Uganda and South Sudan as the month continued. The giant locusts ironically named 'desert locusts' thrive in vegetation caused by heavy rainfall and are usually bound within their natural arid habitats across the Middle East, however an unusually prolonged period of heavy rainfall across Eastern Africa during the previous months resulted in a bloom of vegetation and optimal conditions for the spread of the locusts into the region. The unusual weather conditions were attributed by many to **extreme storm conditions** over the previous months linked to rising ocean temperatures as a result of **Climate Change** affecting the region, a new crisis for the area. These changes in weather potentially offered a sign of the state of things to come as warmer waters and more storms increasingly affect a region already suffering from a plethora of climate related disasters including heavy rainfall and flooding, droughts and desertification amidst political tensions, conflict and the imminent spread of the Coronavirus. The plagues of locusts would go on to affect farming in these already economically fragile nations for the rest of 2020.

Other record-breaking climatic events dominated February, including the **hottest temperature ever recorded in Antarctica**. Rare and **unexpected snows** fell over Baghdad, Iraq as the nation witnessed protests against an ongoing 'ruling elite' with the appointment of new prime minister-designate Mohammed Tawfiq Allawi.

Whilst extreme weather events are not always welcome, **extreme flood-inducing rainfall** was warmly received in New South Wales, Australia where numerous bushfires raging through the state throughout January were finally put to an end. The

worst rains in 30 years to hit the coastal state brought wide-spread flash flooding affecting over 100,000 homes yet putting an end to over 30 wildfires that had been terrorizing the region.

Aside from such extreme, record-breaking climatic threats to our planet, February 2020, continued to show the world, that the human being is not only vulnerable to threat but can in turn threaten the lives of many.

A community of Nigerian travellers settled down for the night in their vehicles alongside a highway near Auno town, north-eastern Nigeria on February 7th. Most were taking an overnight stop in their motors on the long journey to the capital of Borno State, Maiduguri. During the early hours, militants in trucks mounted with heavy weapons, looted the vehicles and torched them, resulting in the **deaths of over 30 people and the complete destruction of 18 vehicles**. State governor, Babagana Zutum to so view the charred remains of the victims of this Sunday night attack and confirmed that the abduction of women and children had also taken place. Militant attacks in northern Nigeria, were becoming less frequent as the government increasingly gained influence over terrorist groups such as Boko Haram, but this horrific tragedy was a clear reminder of the unstable situation in the country which has cost over 35,000 lives over the past decade. However, Nigeria was not the only country to provide victims to the human extremist in February.

The following day Thailand celebrated Makha Bucha Day, an important Buddhist festival which marks the historical moment where the Lord Buddha was visited under a full moon by 1250 enlightened disciples. The day was also marked by **Thailand's deadliest shooting in its history**. As traditional festivities took place across most of the country, Thai soldier Jakraphanth Thomma shot dead his commanding officer and his commanding officer's mother-in-law, before visiting a large shopping mall and posting live updates on social media of his shooting spree which resulted in the deaths of 30 victims and ultimately himself. On the way to the shopping mall, Thomma fired shots at a Buddhist temple, before arriving at the mall, shooting indiscriminately at shoppers, taking sixteen hostages and live streaming the entire event on Facebook. Motivated by anger at a failed financial deal with his colonel, Thomma was heard during his live stream shouting 'Rich from cheating and taking advantage of people… do they think they can take money to spend in hell?'. Thomma's mother was brought to the shopping mall to try and convince her son to release the hostages and at 09:13am on the 9th February, the perpetrator was shot dead by police.

Within days of the African highway burnings and the Asian shooting spree, another headline-hitting massacre reached the news screens of Europe; the murder of 10 innocent lives in Hanau, a small town near the German city of Frankfurt.

At 10pm, on the 19th February 2020, right wing extremist Tobias Rathjen, 43, approached two shisha bars in Hanau's central square and **shot down eight customers and a waiter** before returning home and turning the gun on his own mother and then himself. Rathjen's personal website was found to include extreme political views and it was believed the shooting was a **xenophobic terrorist attack**, with all victims being of non-German origin. The shooting shocked the town of Hanau and a march to show unity towards the victims of the attack was attended by over 10,000 mourners four days later; the same day that a controversial shooting rocked the North American continent.

Ahmaud Arbery was a 25 year old, black man, running in the streets near Brunswick in the state of Georgia on February 23rd, when he was pursued by three white residents, one who was a retired police officer, who believed that Arbery may have been responsible for a series of recent burglaries and trespassing incidents in the area. Identifying Arbery as the suspect, ex-police officer Gregory McMichael and his son Travis mounted their trucks and followed Arbery. A further resident, William Bryan, also followed the chase, recording an altercation between the McMichaels and Arbery from the front seat of his vehicle as he pulled up behind the McMichael's truck. The disturbing video later made global media and showed a struggle, the sound of gunshots and the eventual killing of Arbery by the McMichaels. The incident brought particular international coverage as no arrests were initially made of the McMichael family for their role in the shooting and the incident reignited debates about racial inequality in the United States. A debate which would gain much momentum as 2020 continued.

As the news of fatal shootings in February spread from continent to continent, so did Coronavirus which marked a significant milestone in terms of its international prevalence. The first Coronavirus related death in the United States occurred on February 6th, **South Korea became on high alert** as the death toll from the Covid-19 disease rose to 6. China declared the virus to be the **largest health emergency** the country had faced since the establishment of Mao's communist party in 1949 and declared a two-week lockdown and quarantine in Beijing for residents returning from New Year celebrations. **3700 passengers were detained** near Yokohama, Japan on a virus-infected cruise ship, the 'Diamond Princess' and the virus solidified its position as a **threat to Europe** as the small town of Lombardy in Northern Italy declared an emergency with 152 cases and 3 deaths. By the end of February, the worldwide death toll from Covid-19 related illnesses had surpassed that of the previous Coronavirus related disease, SARS, which affected mostly Asia in 2003.

February ended with the additional leap year date of the 29th, a date which may prove to be one of the most promising additions to 2020, a day which provided some hope for the people of Afghanistan as the US and Taliban signed a deal to end a conflict which had ravaged the nation for 18 years.

Spring 2020:

Locked-Down and Locked-Up

The first case of Coronavirus in New York was diagnosed on March 1, the month in which the world would begin locking down its cities and borders in an attempt to control the spread of a virus which was to now be declared a **global pandemic** by the World Health Organisation. With Iran and Italy as global pandemic hotspots, Iran attempted to reduce infections within its prisons by temporarily **releasing 54,000 prisoners** who had sentences of less than five years. Italy responded with a local lockdown of the Lombardy epicentre on the 8th March, only to follow with a **national Lockdown** the next day as cases rocketed to over 10,000 with almost 700 deaths. Italy had quickly become the world's leading centre of the outbreak as global cases outside China outstripped the number of cases identified within China itself. The president of the United States declared a national emergency in the second week of March and banned travel in and out of the US as well as **closing the border to Canada.** Lockdowns began in countries across the world including in large populous countries such as Nigeria and India. By the 24th March, all 1.3 billion Indians had entered a **21-day lockdown** as the nation tried to prevent the virus reaching areas of extreme poverty which could push the number of infections into the millions. Spain became the country with the second highest number of infections after Italy and the United Kingdom entered its own lockdown on the 15th August. Ten days later the British Royal Family reported that Prince Charles, the **Prince of Wales, had contracted the virus**, an announcement which came right before **British Prime Minister Boris Johnson also tested positive** for Covid-19. Johnson made an address to the British people that he was feeling well and able to continue leading the country remotely during his isolation due to the 'wizardry' of modern technology.

This was the month where the world began to realise the extent of the challenge ahead and accept the pandemic as a global challenge now affecting millions and their livelihoods. Lockdowns inevitably meant less spending in societies which in turn suggested that significant job losses and risks to the future of businesses were on the horizon. As Iran unlocked its doors to prisoners and most of the world entered lock down scenarios, one of the world's leading film producers was preparing to face being locked-up for the next 23 years.

Born in New York to a Jewish family in 1952, Harvey Weinstein went on to create the American entertainment company Miramax with his brother when he was only 27. The company would propel Weinstein's fortunes to dizzy heights as it produced dozens of internationally acclaimed movies, including numerous films exploring sexuality such as 'Sex, Lies, and Videotape; Tie Me Up! Tie Me Down! and 'The Crying Game'. By 2017, the billionaire was accused of numerous counts of **sexually harassing, assaulting, or raping women throughout his career in media**. As a criminal investigation was launched and his wife announced her application to divorce the media mogul, a global movement of women coming forward to report sexual harassment took social media by storm. The #metoo hashtag gained momentum with not only ordinary civilians but highly influential celebrities sharing their own mistreatment within the American television and film industry. Weinstein was finally found guilty of counts of sexual assault and rape. On March 11th, 2020 he was **sentenced to 23 years in prison**. During the same month, while incarcerated in a correctional facility in western New York, it was claimed that Weinstein tested positive for Covid-19, although this was later disputed after he had shown no signs of any symptoms. Days before Weinstein's sentencing, on March 20th, India's justice system dealt with their own high profile case of sexual attacks against women and **hung four men** who had been sentenced by the Supreme Court to the death penalty for sexual attacks that had occurred eight years previously in 2012. Speaking on behalf of women who had been sexually mistreated, the Indian Prime

Minister said, 'justice has prevailed'. Weinstein on the other hand remains locked-up in the United States considering an appeal to his sentencing. In contrast to these criminals who had received a curtailing of their life through either death or imprisonment, it was in March 2020 that Russia's highest court announced changes to the Russian constitution which would enable **Vladimir Putin to remain as president for the rest of his life**, rather than be bound by term limits which were previously in place. This announcement in Putin's favour came days after the president shared other proposals for changes to the constitution including an outright **constitutional ban on gay marriage.**

With global lockdowns in place, the world's sporting organisations announced the inevitable; the postponing or cancelling of major national and international sporting events. The PGA, Elite Football, USEFA, French Open, UK Pro Football were all formally postponed as well as an eventual announcement from Japanese Prime Minister Shinzo Abe that the very much anticipated **Tokyo 2020 Olympics would be rescheduled for the summer of 2021**.

A month after the shooting of Armaud Arbery in Georgia, USA by a retired police officer, the race debate was set alight following the **killing of Breonna Taylor** in the US state of Kentucky. Ms

Taylor, who was a black, emergency medical technician was shot in her home by plain clothed police officers who forced their way into her home. They had obtained a warrant to search Breonna's home in response to a suggestion that her previous boyfriend may be hiding drugs in the property. The three police officers who broke down the door of the property found Breonna in bed with her partner shortly after midnight. Not knowing who had broken into the property, Ms Taylor's boyfriend fired a shot at the police officers who intruded into the bedroom unexpectedly. A bullet struck an officer in the leg. The three officers then retaliated with 32 rounds of fire with the resulting death of Breonna. Media reports of rapidly increasing tensions between the American black community and white police officers exacerbated after the event, particularly as numerous errors in the police investigation came to light, including notes in a report that the deceased Breonna Taylor had received 'no injuries'.

March ended with the release of global meteorological data reporting on the previous winter, a winter which once again was breaking records in its climate extremity. As Tennessee suffered **25 deaths in an unusual storm** event and **landslides and heavy rain killed a further 18 in Sao Paulo** Brazil, the UK recorded its **wettest February** since 1862 and Moscow its **warmest winter** season in 140 years. Winter was now over and the world was looking for some hope in the Spring.

Death and Disinfectant

The 1st of April is celebrated in many countries as 'April Fool's Day', a day in which people, enjoy setting pranks on their friends and colleagues. In recent times even the formal media generates false stories for this tradition. Unfortunately, the media headlines of April 1st, 2020, as alarming as they were, were not all jovial. The month began with the **cancelling of further sporting events**, namely the Mens Open Golf Championships and Wimbledon; events which had ran continuously without interruption since World War 2. The United States opened the month with reports of another **6 million unemployment** claims within a one-week period and the global Coronavirus pandemic had now surpassed a million infections with a death toll of more than 51,500. Brazil saw a rapid increase in Covid-19 related deaths, with **more than 1000 per cases in a single day** at the start of April as the Brazilian leader, Jair Bolsanaro, played down the virus by referring to it as 'a little flu'.

It was in April that the first range of economic projections for the rest of the year were released and these were expectedly alarming. The World Trade Organisation released data which suggested an expected **downturn in global trade of up to 32%,** whilst the IMF predicted a global contraction in economic growth of 3%, the **worst since the Great**

Depression of the 1930s. Donald Trump responded to figures released by the WTO by accusing them of **'severely mismanaging'** the world's fight against what he referred to as the 'China Virus'. Later in the month he announced a US freeze on funding to the organisation which he believed received an unfair amount of funding from the US.

In the UK, Queen Elizabeth, gave a televised address, only her 5th in her reign outside of the usual Christmas message. She gave thanks to all those working on the front line, particularly the National Health Service and tried to reassure her subjects that the virus will soon be overcome if we remain 'united and resolute'. The only other times in her 68-year reign she had addressed the public directly were for the start of Gulf War preparations in 1991, the death of Princess Diana in 1997, the death of the Queen Mother in 2002 and for her own Diamond Jubilee in 2012.

On the other side of the globe, the forces of nature were once again in play and this time wreaking havoc on communities already trying to deal with the virus. On the 2nd of April, passengers on board the MV Taimareho, a passenger boat in the Solomon Islands were trying to return to their home villages following evacuation as a result of **coronavirus evacuation plans**. During sail, the ferry was subject to the effects of Cyclone Harold, the first Category 5 storm of 2020. **28 people were swept overboard**, and the captain was heavily criticised for underplaying warning signals issued by the meteorological agencies. Power lines were brought down across the Solomon Islands and buildings had their roofs removed. Many residents took shelter inside caves to protect themselves against the 235km/h winds.

Despite the global struggle against the virus which in some cases appeared to be uniting nations against a common enemy, April was once again the fourth in as many months of 2020 where a lack of empathy for others resulted in another fatal massacre by gunfire. This time, the shooting was in Canada.

On April 18th, Gabriel Wortman **set fires at numerous locations** across Nova Scotia and **shot down dead 22 civilians** before being shot himself by police. The shooting was the deadliest recorded in Canadian history. Unlike the attacks in the earlier months of 2020, this massacre began as the result of a domestic argument between Wortman and his girlfriend as they celebrated an anniversary at a party. After taking his partner home, tying her up and **setting fire to the house with her inside**, he returned to the party where they had spent the evening and opened fire. The evening events then followed with Wortman going on a violent rampage of his local community impersonating a police officer himself and leaving 8 more victims to die in numerous house fires he started. The Canadian leadership immediately condemned the attacks and swiftly paved the way to consider new laws on rifle ownership.

The leadership of countries was pedantically scrutinised as April drew to a close, with various leaders approaching the challenges the year had brought them in different ways. Some regions saw the positive effects of lock downs on reducing the spread of the virus whilst other regions, saw increases. South Korea celebrated their first day with no new recorded cases of the virus, hailed as the impact of superb leadership by the ruling party who were also re-elected in April by an online voting process which saw the leadership win with an election landslide. A promising end of the month to a nation, only to be overshadowed by the **deaths of 39 people at a construction site** in Icheon as a result of a fire which took place on a building site which did not have obligatory safety measures in place.

In the US, April ended with a different style of leadership. Donald Trump was lambasted by physicians at home and abroad after apparently suggesting whether **injecting disinfectant** into the body or **irradiating patients** with UV lights would be possible options for treating the virus. His comments came after research presented to the White House showed that heat, light and indeed bleach could kill the virus. The US Centre for Disease Control and Prevention responded to the president's comments by warning Americans to be careful with clearing products, acknowledging that calls to poison centres had increased sharply. The US Food and Drug

Administration also warned strongly against ingesting disinfectants and bogus miracle cures purporting to treat everything from autism to AIDS.

The Swedish leadership of the virus was being closely monitored to see the impact of their more controversial policy of herd immunity and strategies which relied on individuals to take responsibility for their own social distancing whilst maintaining an open economy. In the UK, leadership of the virus was distributed amongst cabinet members as Boris Johnson began recovering from his time spent in **intensive care on a ventilator** as the UK death toll climbed towards 30,000.

Rule Breakers

As parts of Europe slowly eased lockdown restrictions, there were calls for an inquiry into the handling of the pandemic in the UK as the four-nation state confirmed over 32,000 coronavirus related deaths, **the highest toll of any country in Europe.** This news came in tandem with Bank of England forecasts predicting the **worse economic crises ahead for the UK since 1706.** The speed in which the UK originally responded to the virus was questioned. Per capita, the death rate in the UK climbed to the fourth worst in Europe with 43.3 deaths per 100,000 people compared to 69.4 in Belgium. Deaths in care homes were seen to count for a significant proportion of the increased toll.

The UK government was under further scrutiny, when on 24th May, British newspapers revealed that senior advisor to Prime Minister Boris Johnson, had made journeys outside his home during the national lockdown. According to the press, on the same day that Johnson had been diagnosed with Covid-19, Cummings had suspected that his family may have the virus. Concerned as to who would take care of their four-year old son if they were taken ill, the family drove from London to Durham to stay at a house near his parents. The visit also included an additional 30-mile family drive to Barnard Castle. The news of this investigation was met with widespread calls from the public and Members of Parliament for Cummings to resign having breached the guidance that the government was enforcing during lockdown. Cumming's was interrogated live on television and part of his justification for his **breach of lockdown rules,** was a need to drive to Barnard Castle to 'test his eyesight and his capability to drive. The incident was seen as a **national embarrassment** for the UK government, particularly as Johnson refused to dismiss Cummings for his actions. Cummings would later leave his post unexpectedly in November, with reports of 'turmoil' within the Prime Minister's office.

In May, figures released estimated that more than **90,000 health care workers across the globe were now infected** with the virus. Africa also became the next continent to confirm that **all its nations had cases** of Coronavirus; Lesotho being the final country to declare their first infection. In the United States, Donald Trump claimed he had started taking the **anti-malarial drug hydroxychloroquine** to protect against infection from the virus. No evidence existed that the drug would be an effective preventative measure against infection and virologists were quick to share with the media that any limited trials of the drug and its role in coronavirus had been largely inconclusive, Donald Trump, remained very optimistic that the drug would protect him and it is not known whether he was taken the drug regularly in the run up to his eventual infection with the virus.

Tensions between the US and China continued to be fierce as during the month of May, the US administration and Trump himself regularly **accused China of 'mass worldwide killing'**, even suggesting that the virus was man-made and leaked from a lab in Wuhan, China in January. The Chinese foreign ministry responded to the US allegations as **'lies and rumors'.**

Global businesses were feeling the pressure of recent closures and trade remained low for many. As airlines across the world suffered significant losses due to bans on international air travel, the second oldest airline in the world, Colombian based **Avianca, filed for bankruptcy**, the first major airline to do so in 2020. Citing an 80% cut in income since the pandemic began, it was also struggling with high fixed costs. **20,000 jobs across Latin America** were threatened by the motion.

Other than the pandemic, arguably one of the most significant events of May 2020, occurred on May 25th in Minneapolis. George Floyd, a 46-year-old black man was arrested on suspicion of spending counterfeit money. He was arrested by white officer Derek Chauvin, who **knelt on Floyd's neck for almost ten minutes** during the arrest. Video footage emerged of Floyd calling out that he was unable to breath and expressing fear for his life. Chauvin did not remove his knee from Floyd's neck until medics told him to do so. Three other white officers were witness to the arrest and failed to intervene in response to Floyd's distress. Floyd was **pronounced dead at the scene**. Following on from previous deaths of black individuals by white police officers earlier in the year, in Georgia and Kentucky, the news of George Floyd's death sparked worldwide protests against police brutality, racism and absence of accountability. The four officers present during Floyd's death were all dismissed with a criminal court case being expected in March 2021.

May would be the fifth month of the year with significant shootings across the world. The US saw **no fewer than sixty separate shooting sprees** within the one month alone. There was also a particularly violent series of insurgent **attacks in Afghanistan**, where a peace deal between the Taliban and government should now have been in place. On May 12th, a hospital's maternity ward in Kabul was attacked by shooters, alongside a funeral parlour, resulting in the **deaths of 56 people and 150 injuries**. The Afghan government immediately accused the Taliban of the attacks and began to resume its offensives against the Taliban, despite the Taliban's denial of any involvement in the hospital shootings. In retaliation of this accusation, the Taliban then conducted a series of suicide bombings which killed a further 14 individuals and made a failed attempt to capture the city of Kunduz, resulting in further fatalities.

As mother nature appeared much more lenient in her revenge against the human population in May, with much fewer fatalities due to natural disasters than previous months of 2020, human error would still cause accidental and unnecessary loss of lives.

A **gas leak at a chemical factory** in Visakhapatnam, India led to 800 victims being hospitalized and thousands affected. The leak from a polymer factory came at 3am in the early hours of the morning as people slept, leading to residents breathing in toxic gases during the night. At least **86 residents were on hospital ventilators** the next day. Patients reported burning sensations in their eyes and severe difficulties breathing. Legal action was taken against the company who believed that negligence and absence of correct safety procedures in place were at fault when the South-Korean owned factory was reopened following lockdown.

On May 22nd, residents of Karachi watched in horror as they witnessed scheduled domestic flight 8303, Pakistan International Airlines, **crash into their rooftops**. The flight travelling from Lahore, a 90-minute journey, was an A320 Airbus craft which crashed in a densely populated residential area during landing, only a few kilometers from the runaway. Of the 99 people on board, **97 were killed along with a further 8 people on the ground**. Witnesses reported the wings of the craft ablaze in flames moments before the plane came down into the rooftops of a crowded neighbourhood. The crash on the approach to the runaway came after the plane had already made a previous failed attempt to land and had to recircle and try once more. Reports in Indian newspapers claimed that the pilots had ignored warnings from air traffic control regarding the speed and altitude of the plane as it was coming into land. Human error and 'overconfidence' on the part of the pilot were claimed to have led to this fateful event, although the investigation will go on into 2021. The incident caused many across the world to question the pilot training process that occurs as airlines slowly return to flying after widespread lockdowns and international travel bans.

Summer 2020: Protest

Donald Trump was briefly moved to the White House bunker on the 1st June as **protests** continued to take place outside the White House in response to the murder of George Floyd the previous month. The protests which began in Minneapolis, spread to over 2000 cities and towns in over 60 countries as people went to show their support for the 'Black Lives Matter' movement. Most protests were peaceful, however there were some notable protests in the US which were reduced **to riots and looting,** with police and counter-protesters in conflict with protesters. In early June hundreds of cities in the United States **had imposed curfews** to bring an end to the protests and Washington D.C. employed over 60,000 National Guard personnel to support the mass unrest. President Trump declared himself the 'president of law and order' and suggested he would use **military force** if necessary to put an end to the protests. As new information emerged that the black population of the United States were also four times more likely to end up in hospital than the white people due to

Coronavirus, racial tensions increased further. A representative of the United Nations claimed that the virus had certainly revealed the **'economic inequalities'** within societies and former US Defense Secretary, James Mattis, denounced Trump for his leadership and suggestions of militarization to ease protests. Mattis stated 'Trump is the first president in my lifetime who does not try to unite the American people…. Instead he tries to divide us'.

As the BLM movement gained increasing momentum, protesters across the world sought to remove statues of historical figures who were believed to represent colonialism or white supremacy. In Virginia, four **historic monuments were beheaded by protesters** including a statue of Confederate President Jefferson Davis. Across the pond in the UK, British protesters in Bristol pulled down a statue of the historic slave trader Edward Colston by attaching a rope the monument before pulling it to the ground as crowds cheered. The scene drew parallels with the famous topping of the statue of Saddam Hussein in Iraq in 2003.

As the month began with wide-spread protests in the US and beyond for the Black Lives Matter movement, other protesters were making significant political statements in Hong Kong. **Thousands of Hong Kong residents defied a police ban** to mourn the victims of the Chinese Tiananmen Square Massacre and went into the streets to protest. The Tiananmen

Square massacre occurred in 1989 when the Chinese communist government launched military action to end protests in the square by mostly students. Reports claim between hundreds or perhaps thousands of innocent protesters were murdered in the military response to end the protests. The pro-democracy protesters killed by the Chinese government in 1989 have been honoured annually in Hong Kong, one of the few places this has been authorised as China has sought to erase this piece of history. For the first time, Hong Kong authorities, increasingly under the influence of Chinese leadership refused to permit the candlelight vigil to take place in June 2020, citing mass gatherings as restricted under Coronavirus social distancing laws. The ban was breached by thousands of Hongkongers who gathered anyway outside of Victoria Park.

With an ongoing trend of protest movements across the globe in June 2020, it was poignant that this was also the month which Philippines journalist Maria Ressa was found **guilty of 'cyber libel'**. A move which was described as a politically motivated attack on the free press by Philippines Duterte government. The charges against Ressa referred to news publications by her online outlet, 'Rappler', which in 2012 wrote a story about prolific Filipino businessmen having links to **illegal drugs and human trafficking**. Although the article was published two years before Philippine laws came in to affect which banned such investigative journalism which could be construed as 'libel', a correction made to the article since the law was imposed was deemed by the court to constitute its 'republishing' and therefore Ressa was found guilty of 'cyber libel'. The freedom of the Philippine press has been significantly reduced under the leadership of President Duterte and Ressa, who was previously nominated as TIME Magazine Person of the Year, believes her charge was purely politically motivated in order to keep a tight lid on press freedoms within the Philippines.

In a reportedly homophobic protest later in the summer, three **men were brutally murdered in a park** in Reading, England on Saturday June 20th, as they were stabbed by Libyan passer-by Khairi Saadallah. The victims, two of which were reported as 'openly gay and proud' were murdered in an attack which was claimed to not have been pre-meditated but likely as a response to their homosexuality. Saadallah also attempted to murder three others who were sitting within the group. The investigation into the real motive for the attack continues.

June 2020 was a month where global divisions between ideologies, wealth and race felt more prevalent than ever. Aside from wide-scale protests June witnessed other tragedies as a result of large economic inequalities, including the **drowning at sea of 45 economic migrants** fleeing northern Africa via Tunisia in an attempt to reach Italy. China and India saw a violent face-off along their border, the first in many years, resulting in the **deaths of over 20**

soldiers. Meanwhile, New Delhi faced a mile-long swarm of **locusts flying through metro stations** and children's playgrounds in an environmental disaster, referred to as 'Swarmageddon' which Indian officials had been struggling to control for weeks.

One of the most significant events of Summer 2020 other than the obvious global pandemic disaster was an event in Lebanon in August. A **devastating explosion at a port in Beirut** which once again revealed the travesty of human error.

Waiting for Justice:

Beirut, the capital of Lebanon, a city in turmoil, dealing with economic recession, hyper-inflation which had eradicated the savings of many, and the ongoing 2020 battle with Covid-19 was rocked to its core on the 4th August, 2020. Footage released to the world's media networks showed the terrifying scenes as an explosion in the Beirut Port area released enough energy to power 100 homes for more than a year and was one of the largest non-nuclear explosions ever recorded in history. Volunteers in the streets began lifting dead bodies from sites levelled by the explosion and hospitals, already struggling with Covid-19 admissions were put on high alert to receive an unprecedented influx of more than 6500 injured citizens.

The explosion obliterated the Beirut dockside and shaped a crater in the earth 140 metres wide which immediately began to flood with incoming sea water. Ships once anchored in the Mediterranean Sea were now sitting on the dockside having been catapulted by the blast onto the land. Cultural heritage buildings, businesses, educational facilities and infrastructure networks sustained significant damage leading to estimated physical damage costs of almost $5 billion and economic losses close to $3.5 billion.

Following the explosion which shocked the world, Lebanese President, Michel Aoun vowed to hold to account whoever was responsible for the tragedy which ultimately led to over 200 deaths and more than 300,000 homeless individuals.

Shortly after 18:00 local time on the 4th August 2020, a fire broke out at Warehouse 12 at the Port of Beirut on the city's northern Mediterranean cost. The warehouse was adjacent to the storage site of Beirut's largest holdings of grain silos. The fire took hold on the roof of the warehouse creating an initial minor explosion, followed by a series of blasts which eyewitnesses reported as looking and sounding like 'fireworks going off'. Less than a minute since the first explosion, the city was rocked as a colossal explosion occurred at the site, sending a supersonic blast across the city and a mushroom cloud, not dissimilar to the clouds created by the atomic bombs which hit Japan in 1945, was cast spectacularly into the air.

Warehouse 12 had been undergoing maintenance and welding had been conducted on a hole on one of the main doors shortly before the first fire had been ignited on the roof. Stored inside the warehouse was 2,750 tonnes of ammonium nitrate, a highly flammable chemical compound when mixed with other materials. The compound, a crystal=like white solid, is often used as an agricultural fertilizer but also has a function in the construction industry as an explosive to support with the detonation and controlled destruction of building sites. Usually, it can be stored quite safely, yet poses an increased risk the greater the time it is left decaying in storage. This particular stock of ammonium nitrate had been held in the warehouse since 2013 after being confiscated from a Moldovan cargo-ship which when inspected following a technical failure in port was found to be housing the compound, brought into the country illegally. Warehouse 12 had been chosen as an appropriate storage site following a court order with instructions for the stock to be disposed or resold. The chemical was found to have never been properly disposed or removed from the Warehouse, despite senior Lebanese officials reportedly knowing of its presence for over six years. TV journalist, Dima Sadek shared photographs online which reportedly show hundreds of sacks of ammonium nitrate stored carelessly in the warehouse, photographs claimed to have been taken only days before the explosion. Both media networks and locals were quick to point the finger at the Lebanese government officials for having a blatant disregard for public safety by leaving the bags stored insecurely for so long, a further criticism of a government dogged with political turmoil and accusations of deeply embedded corruption. Committees and judges were aware that the material was a risk to the city of Beirut, yet no action had been taken to remove the stock.

Mass protests by citizens against the government's leadership grew momentum in the days after the explosion and desecrated sites were graffitied with anti-government sentiment such as 'our government did this'. Six days later, Prime Minister Hassan Diab announced the resignation of his government citing deep-rooted corruption within the Lebanese system making it impossible to implement reforms to improve the country. The President vowed to hold to account those responsible and enabled Fadi Sawan, a 60-year old military judge to lead the investigation into the incident. An investigation which would potentially expose the negligence of dozens of security, administrative and political officials who failed to act and remove the known, ultimately destructive chemical store.

Public Works Minister Michel Najjar was questioned as part of the investigation. In interview, the minister claimed he did have knowledge of the storage in Warehouse 12 previous to the explosion taking place but had only become aware of the situation within the fortnight leading up to the tragedy. He confirmed that he had spoken to the general manager of the port the day before the blast asking him to investigate the situation. The Director of Lebanese Customs told media he had contacted the Lebanese Judiciary numerous times and had presented them with several documents warning about the dangers of the stored material. He had explicitly requested for the ammonium nitrate to be re-exported, yet no action was taken by the Judiciary.

By September, a month after the investigation had been launched, Amnesty International called for an international fact-finding mission to replace Sawan's investigation which had so far produced statements which failed to hold senior officials to account, an investigation accused of avoiding transparency, impartiality and the rights of victims to truth, justice and remedy. International support was given to Sawan's investigative team and by mid-October, Lebanon received a report from the American FBI's own investigation into the devastating blast. Lebanon requested Interpol to arrest two people who were allegedly responsible for bringing the original shipment into Lebanon in 2013 and 25 were arrested and detained in Beirut including port and customs officials along with military officers. As of October 2020, the final findings of the FBI report and work by other international investigators such as French and British explosive experts have not been shared, nor has any sentencing taken place. Officials close to the FBI report were claimed to have leaked information to the media suggesting that the final report findings show the explosion to have been a deliberate attack and not an accident, yet the FBI were quick to deny this. The people of Lebanon remain in waiting for justice.

Autumn 2020

In another 2020 event of racial controversy, the month of August 2020 ended with the **shooting of Jacob S. Blake,** a 29-year-old African American in the state of Wisconsin, USA. The shooting followed a call to state police by a woman who claimed that Blake had stolen her key. Blake was currently being sought by police for claims that he had sexually assaulted her in July. With knowledge of Blake's location, officers sought down a **knife-wielding Blake** and attempted to subdue him with tasers. Witnesses claim they did not see Blake carrying any weapon although they did hear police requests for Blake to 'put a knife down'. One of the officers present saw Blake put a child into a car and attempt to drive off with it. The woman who had contacted the police about Blake called to police that Blake was **stealing her child** as well as her keys. In order to detain Blake, he was shot at seven times. Four of the bullets seriously wounding him. Blake was later **declared paralysed from the waist down** with damage to his stomach, kidney and liver. The incident re-launched some of the protests for Black Lives Matter that had occurred in Wisconsin previously and further marches rallies and damage by rioters to property then followed. Only days after this event, video footage of the **killing by police officers of a black man, Daniel Prude** in March came to light revealing his murder by white police officers in New York. Daniel, a 41-year-old African-American had been suffering a mental health episode and was wandering through the streets of New York **naked and spitting**. Video evidence shows that Prude was detained with a spitting-hood put over his neck before being **held down on the pavement until he stopped breathing**. Following the release of this video evidence in September, protests against race inequality continued to exacerbate in the United States.

Coronavirus cases continued to rise throughout August and September and many nations that had lifted lockdowns were contemplating a second. The WHO estimated that at least **10% of the world's population** may now have been infected with the virus and India reported positive tests for 6.6 million people, with the third highest death toll after the US and Brazil. On October 2nd President Donald Trump and his wife, First Lady, Melania Trump confirmed they had **tested positive for COVID-19** and the president was later hospitalised that day. By the 5th October, he had left hospital and returned to the White House, **despite still being infectious**. Many European nations began setting curfews for their populations, rather than full lockdowns whilst the UK proposed a new three tier system of Coronavirus response. Following claims that New Zealand was now free of Coronavirus, Labour Party leader Jacinda Ardern was re-elected Prime Minister in a landslide victory in the 2020 New Zealand general election. By the end of the month, many countries had **re-implemented lockdowns**, including the UK who announced a second four-week lockdown for England, with schools, universities, and essential services to remain open.

Natural Hazards didn't leave the world alone in the Autumn. **Vietnam suffered its worst floods in decades** with the Red Cross reporting over 100 deaths and the displacement of 90,000 people across the Hue Province. The intense rainfall and flooding were a result of Storms Nangka and Linfa which both hit the country within days of each other. As if Vietnam had not been battered by enough rainfall, only days after these two storms the country was hit by the track Typhoon Molave which **triggered more landslides** and brought another 60 fatalities. In the US, Wildfires broke out in Orange County, forcing **60,000 people to evacuate** and a 7.0 magnitude earthquake in the Aegean Sea **killed over 70 across Turkey and Greece.**

As natural hazards, human error, Coronavirus and racial tension continued their 2020 performance of depressing the world throughout the Autumn, two majorly cruel events occurred in France in October 2020 which unfortunately followed in the footsteps of previous 2020 tragedies: human terrorism.

Samuel Paty was a middle-school teacher working in the suburbs of Paris, France when he was attacked by an 18-year-old refugee and **beheaded with a Clever**. Investigations found that Samuel had shown his students the highly controversial cartoons of the Islamic prophet Muhammad which had previously been published by Charlie Hebdo. The teacher had invited Muslim students to leave the classroom during the discussion, however one of the student's parents took a grievance with the teaching and mobilised other parents to take action against the teacher; ultimately leading to the teacher's beheading by perpetrator Abdullakh Anzorov, on October 16th, who was known by authorities for engaging in radicalised behaviour. Only days later **another attack occurred in France,** this time in Nice.

On October 29th at 08:30 am an attacker entered the Roman Catholic basilica of Notre-Dame de Nice and **killed three people with a knife**. The attacker carried out his violent stabbing spree for 28 minutes whilst shouting 'Allahu Akbar!' The alleged attacker was a 21-year old Tunisian male, who was shot by police who intervened at the crime scene. In December, the alleged attacker recovered from his injuries in hospital and was placed under formal investigation allowing him to be questioned in relation to the knife attack.

Autumn 2020 drew to a close with the election of Joe Biden as President-elect of the United States, a result which is still contested as fraud by outgoing President Donald Trump. It is expected that Biden will take office in January 2021 in what will hopefully be a more positive year for everyone. Newly approved Coronavirus vaccines released in December give hope to all. The world's first person to have the new Pfizer manufactured Covid-19 vaccination was a 91-year-old female Margaret Keenan from Coventry England. She was closely followed by the first man to receive the vaccine, William Shakespeare and it is hoped that as countries bid to obtain supplies of vaccines and distribute these to their populations, 2021 can be a year of hope for the planet.

2020 was a year of misery. Thank GOD its over.

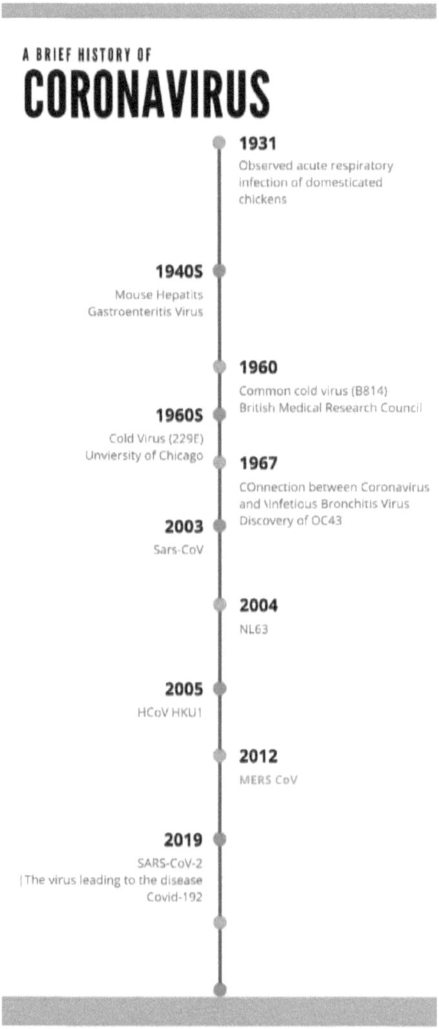
A BRIEF HISTORY OF
CORONAVIRUS
1931
Observed acute respiratory infection of domesticated chickens
1940S
Mouse Hepatits Gastroenteritis Virus
1960
Common cold virus (B814) British Medical Research Council
1960S
Cold Virus (229E) Unviersity of Chicago
1967
COnnection between Coronavirus and \Infetious Bronchitis Virus Discovery of OC43
2003
Sars-CoV
2004
NL63
2005
HCoV HKU1
2012
MERS CoV
2019
SARS-CoV-2
|The virus leading to the disease Covid-192

Bonus Chapter: Where did Coronavirus come from?

The 2020 Coronavirus pandemic is not the first time we have seen Coronavirus threatening our way of life, nor is this virus unique to humans. Chickens, cows and pigs have all been affected by this virus over the last century, leaving these animals with upper tract respiratory infections and diarrhea. In humans, the virus has caused not only widespread illness such as the common cold, but also more lethal varieties of infections including SARS and MERS.

In 1931, farmers in Dakota, North America, were concerned about an infection spreading amongst their chickens. Mortality rate was high, with between 40% and 90% of chickens dying prematurely across different farms in the region. The cause of the widespread chicken culling was identified almost six years after the pattern had started and was identified as a form of bronchitis, affecting the birds' ability to breathe. Chicks, unable to breathe, gasping and listless, were identified at birth and this was all attributed to Infections bronchitis Virus (IBV), an infection later to be discovered as initiated by a Coronavirus. Over the next decade, other animals suffered various forms of misery, including the 1940s, hepatitis virus infecting mice (MHV) and the transmissible gastroenteritis virus (TGEV) which were both isolated and studied. At this time, the connection between all these viruses was not yet understood; the potential of Coronavirus as an multi-infection spawning killer had yet to be uncovered.

It wasn't until the 1960s that the virus began to be better understood. In the early part of the decade, the Common Cold Unit of the British Medical Research Council isolated from a child a novel common cold virus (B814). The scientists cultivated this virus by passing it through human organ culture from the embryonic trachea. The virus was thus identified as the cause of a typical cold like illness. The University of Chicago was similarly working on isolating the virus which caused cold and they performed trials and tests using kidney tissue culture and identified a virus 229E, which similar to the one identified by the British, caused a cold when inoculated into volunteers. Both new strains of virus were subject to electron microscopy at St. Thomas Hospital, London where they were both shown to be morphologically related viruses, distinctive by their club-like spikes. The physical characteristics of the viruses enabled scientists to link them further to Infections Bronchitis Virus (IBV), which had been seen in the chickens of North Dakota in the 1940s. It wasn't long before the Mouse Hepatitis Virus was also proven to be connected and this collection of morphologically similar viruses came to be known as coronavirus due to their distinctive crown like features. Over the next few decades, two human affecting coronaviruses, 229E and OC43 continued to be analysed by scientists and a range of new related coronaviruses were discovered, notable findings include SARS-CoV in 2003, HCoV in 2003, MERS-CoV in 2012 and SARS-CoV-2 in 2019. Further forms of coronavirus affecting animals within global farm populations were also identified.

Attempts have been made to try and identify the true origins of the virus, long before it affected the chickens of North Dakota. There is consensus amongst many scientists that the coronavirus origins date back to 8000 BCE, although there are claims by some that the common ancestor of the virus can be dated back 55 million years or more. Such historical development of the virus suggests that there has been a long=term coevolution of the virus within bats and avian species. As warm-blooded, flying species, capable of harbouring and spreading the virus, bats and birds are an ideal reservoir for the coronavirus gene. It is believed that bats are the origin for many human coronaviruses, although bats are thought not to be the only carrier. The Middle Eastern Respiratory Syndrome, MERS-CoV, causing widespread infection in 2012, whilst believed to have originated from bats, was transferred to humans through camels which acted as intermediate hosts. This MERS-CoV strain of the virus is believed to have diverged from bats several centuries ago, taking host in camels of the Middle East. SARS-CoV, Severe Accute Respiratory Syndrome, famous for causing widespread infection in the early 2000s in Asia, is thought to be more closely related to several coronavirus species found in bats. It is expected that the SARS related viruses coevolved in bats for thousands of years, first infecting leaf-nose bats, spreading to horseshoe bats, evolving into Asian palm civets before eventually transmitting to humans.

There are other forms of Coronavirus that are believed not have their origin in bats at all and are thought to have originated in rodents. The famous global flu pandemic of 1890, known as 'Russian flu' or 'Asian flu', killed over 1 million people and is mistakenly named as a 'flu'. It is speculated that this virus was not the influenza virus at all but by a coronavirus originating in rodents.

There are currently six species of coronavirus known to affect humans, with one of these species being divided into two separate strains. Four of these virus strains produce infections such as the common cold and are not so severe, the other three (SARS-CoV,

MERS-CoV and SARS-CoV-2), produce potentially lethal respiratory infections. The risks from these strains vary greatly with some, such as MERS-CoV killing more than 30% of those infected. Major symptoms such as sore throats, fever and swollen adenoids can result from these viruses as well as leading to pneumonia and bronchitis. Other strains of the virus are relatively harmless, producing the common cold. The 2003 disovery of SARS-CoV, revealed a unique strain of the virus which affects both the lower and upper human respiratory tract causing serious infection.

The human population is riddled with the common cold, yet it is worth noting that not all common colds are caused by coronaviruses. Coronavirus accounts for approximately only 15% of human cold cases, most others being from other viruses such as the Rhinovirus.

The last two decades have seen the global human population significantly affected by the three severe strains of the coronavirus with widespread devastating fatalities.

In 2003, the World Health Organisation (WHO) stated that a novel coronavirus had been identified and was the cause behind the outbreak of severe acute respiratory syndrome across Asia. Moore than 8000 people were infected with this strain with approximately 800 deaths. By September 2012, a new form of the virus was identified, originally called Novel Coronavirus 2012, it was later renamed MERS-CoV, representing the Middle Eastern Respiratory Syndrome. This form of the virus was originally believed to not be able to pass between humans easily, however in May 2013 it was confirmed that human to human transmission had taken place in France and Tunisia. Two of the Tunisian cases involved people who appeared to have caught the disease from their father after he had visited Qatar and Saudi Arabia. Saudi Arabia later identified human to human transmission of this camel-originating virus leading to a total of 52 deaths in the country. The virus was ineffective at causing a global pandemic and cases were rare and not fatal in the US and Europe, however an outbreak of MERS-CoV was reported in the Republic of Korea in 2015 after a man returned with the virus from his travels in the Middle East. To this date, almost 3000 cases of MERS-CoV have been identified over the last two decades with a fatality rate of about 35% of those infected, significantly greater than the mortality rate of the Asian originating SARS-CoV.

At the turn of 2020, a new strain of Coronavirus was circulating in the human society which traces its first known appearance in humans to an outbreak of respiratory illness in Wuhan, China on 31st December 2019. The illness was reported as a pneumonia

outbreak, identified as being caused by a new, novel strain of the virus which the WHO gave the interim name of 2019-nCoV, later renamed by the International Committee on Taxonomy of Viruses as SARS-Cov-2. This strain is what we now know as the cause of the 2020 pandemic. This Wuhan strain has been identified as having 70% genetic similarity to the original SARS-CoV and a 96% similarity to a particular strain of coronavirus which affects bats. Therefore, it is widely suspected that this form also originated from the bat population. The pandemic, resulted in global travel restrictions, social lockdowns and an unprecedented worldwide death toll from respiratory tract
infections caused by the virus.

Due to the rapidly changing nature of information associated with the current virus, we encourage readers to refer to official sources for health information.

'UNPRECEDENTED DECLINE'